Stuart's Moon Suit

by Carol Talley
illustrated by Sean O'Neill

Editorial Offices: Glenview, Illinois • Parsippany, New Jersey • New York, New York
Sales Offices: Needham, Massachusetts • Duluth, Georgia • Glenview, Illinois
Coppell, Texas • Ontario, California • Mesa, Arizona

All Friday afternoon Stuart sat thinking. His mom watched him think. His dad watched him think. Even his sister, Doris, watched Stuart think. What loomed in his mind?

When it was time for dinner, Stuart was still thinking. "Would you like some more macaroni?" asked Stuart's dad. Stuart looked up.

"Neil Armstrong," he said summoning up what was on his mind.

"Neil Armstrong?" asked Doris. "What about Neil Armstrong?"

"Neil Armstrong was the first man on the moon," Stuart said.

"Actually Neil Armstrong and Buzz Aldrin landed on the moon at the same time," said Stuart's mom. "They were both in the lunar module *Eagle* when it touched down on the moon's Sea of Tranquility."

"I mean Neil Armstrong was the first man to walk on the moon," Stuart said. "So, I have decided to be him!"

"You want to walk on the moon?" Stuart's mother asked.

Stuart smiled. "Maybe some day. But right now I just want to make a Neil Armstrong costume for Space Travel Day at school!"

"Space Travel Day is next Monday," Doris said. "Where are you going to find a space suit?" Stuart looked thoughtful again.

"We'll make one!" Stuart exclaimed.

The next afternoon, when Doris trudged in from her violin lesson, Stuart was in his pajamas. "Neil Armstrong did not wear his pajamas on the moon," taunted Doris.

"But he wore something that looked like this! He wore his LCG. That stands for Liquid Cooling Garment. That was the first layer of the Apollo space suit."

"But did Neil Armstrong's cooling garment have grape jelly on the front?" she asked.

"I don't think so," said Stuart, "but the LCG had little plastic tubes all through it. Cool water flowed through the tubes, right next to Armstrong's skin. He stayed cool!"

"Hey," said Doris. "That grape jelly makes me think of something. See you later!"

When Doris came back, she was eating a peanut butter and jelly sandwich. Stuart's dad was fastening shoulder pads onto Stuart.

"Now what?" wondered Doris. "Don't tell me Neil Armstrong played football on the moon!"

"Nope," said Stuart. "Astronauts didn't wear football gear on the moon. But on top of their Liquid Cooling Garment, they wore a PGA."

"A what?" Doris asked.

"PGA stands for Pressure Garment Assembly," said Stuart. "It's clothing that protects the astronauts from outer space."

"I'll explain," said Stuart's mom. "On Earth, even though we can't feel it, the air presses against our bodies from all directions. But there's no air on the moon. That's called a vacuum. And we can't live in a vacuum."

"If Neil Armstrong was in a vacuum," Stuart said, "the air inside his lungs would escape into space. The oxygen in his blood would bubble. His skin would blow up like a balloon!"

"That's horrible!" squealed Doris.

"That's outer space," said Stuart. "The Pressure Garment Assembly is like an inflated tire inside the space suit. It presses against the astronaut's body like air pressure does here on Earth. It feels like wearing a diving suit over football pads!"

"Well, Stuart, so far you don't look like an Apollo astronaut," said Doris. "You look like the runt of the NFL."

"Just wait, Doris," said Stuart. "Hey, Mom! How are we coming with my Integrated Thermal Micrometeoroid Garment?"

"Your what?" Doris asked.

"Hey," she added. "This looks like my old bedspread!"

"It was your old bedspread," said Stuart. "Now it's an ITMG! Neil Armstrong's Integrated Thermal Micrometeoroid Garment! This protected him from all kinds of danger. Do you know how hot it gets on the moon?"

"Wait, isn't the moon cold?" Doris asked. "Now I'm really confused!"

"When it is dark on the moon's surface, it can be as cold as 240 degrees below zero," Stuart said. "But when the sun is shining, the temperature rises to almost 250 degrees above zero! That's really hot!"

Stuart touched his suit. "But it's no problem with this ITMG! It's made of eighteen layers of space-age material. And it's insulated!"

"Like oven mitts?" asked Doris.

"This ITMG also would protect against micrometeoroids," Stuart said. "Those are small bits of rock and metal that zip through space and hit the moon. Larger meteors that slam into the moon can make a long trench, or rille. If one had torn a hole in Neil Armstrong's pressurized spacesuit, it would have been a disaster. But they can't rip through the ITMG."

Just then, Stuart's dad rushed into the room carrying a pair of big white boots.

"I spray-painted these, Stuart," his dad said. "What do you think?"

"Hey, are those my galoshes?" exclaimed Stuart's mom.

"They're lunar boots now!" Stuart exclaimed, pulling on the boots. "Neil Armstrong's boots had an outer layer of woven metal. They protected his feet from moon rocks. Twenty-five layers of insulation kept his feet cool on the hot surface of the moon."

"And here are your lunar gloves," said Stuart's dad. Stuart pulled them on.

"Rubber gloves?" questioned Doris.

"Real space gloves would be airtight and pressurized. They'd fit my hand like a second skin," Stuart said. "These gloves protect astronauts' hands from the heat, cold, and even rough moon rocks!"

"You know what?" said Doris. "You are beginning to look sort of like an astronaut!"

"Thanks, Doris," said Stuart, "but my moon suit's not finished yet!"

It was late afternoon when Doris looked in on the lunar space suit team again.

Now Stuart was wearing a white box on his back, and his mom was gluing red and blue bottle caps to the front of his space suit.

"Just in time, Doris," said Stuart. "We're about to plug in the connections for my PLSS!

"Your PLSS?" asked Doris.

"My Portable Life Support System," said Stuart. "The PLSS gives an astronaut oxygen to breathe. The oxygen also kept Armstrong's suit pressurized when he did his moon walk. The PLSS made him feel comfortable because it kept cool water flowing in his suit. The PLSS also had a system that let him talk to Buzz Aldrin and to Mission Control on Earth.

"Is your moon suit finished now?" Doris asked.

"Almost," said Stuart. "Shut your eyes." Doris did. "Now open them!"

Doris stared at Stuart. He had on a space helmet!

"Mom," said Doris, "that looks like our big plastic fruit bowl."

"It is." said Stuart's mom. "Doesn't Stuart look good?" she said as Stuart staggered around in his new moon suit.

"Good?" Doris replied. "I'd say he looks amazing!"

Apollo 11 to the Moon

On July 16, 1969, the *Apollo 11* spacecraft was launched from the Kennedy Space Center in Florida. *Apollo 11* traveled three days and then went into orbit around the moon. On July 20, Neil Armstrong and Buzz Aldrin climbed into a smaller ship, the lunar module *Eagle,* and went to the moon's surface. When they touched down on the Sea of Tranquility, Armstrong radioed Mission Control in Texas and said, "Houston, Tranquility Base here. The Eagle has landed."

People around the world were glued to their TV sets. They watched as Armstrong climbed out of the *Eagle* and stepped down onto the moon. While astronaut Michael Collins orbited above in *Columbia*, Armstrong and Aldrin took photographs, collected rock and soil samples, and set up scientific instruments. They left a plaque that says, "Here men from the planet Earth first set foot upon the Moon." When they had completed their work, the men returned to *Columbia* and headed home.